This book is dedicated to all aspiring entrepreneurs who dream of launching their own social media marketing agency but are held back by financial constraints.

To those of you who believe that money is the only way to start a successful business, we hope to inspire you to think outside the box and find creative ways to make your dreams a reality.

To the brave souls who are willing to take a leap of faith, put in the hard work, and invest in themselves and their future, we commend you.

May this book provide you with the tools, knowledge, and confidence to break free from financial limitations and launch your very own social media marketing agency for free.

We wish you all the best on this exciting journey and look forward to seeing you thrive in the world of social media marketing!

Sincerely,

Tushar Raj

Made with ♥ on the Notion Press Platform
www.notionpress.com

LAUNCH YOUR FREE SOCIAL MEDIA AGENCY: BREAKING GROUND

TUSHAR RAJ

Contents

Foreword

Welcome to "Launch Your Free Social Media Agency: Breaking Ground"! This book is designed for anyone who is interested in starting their own social media marketing agency but doesn't want to break the bank. In today's digital age, social media marketing has become an essential tool for businesses to connect with their customers, increase their brand awareness, and boost their sales. As a result, the demand for social media marketing services is constantly increasing, making it a great time to start your own agency.

However, starting a social media marketing agency can be daunting, especially if you have limited resources. The good news is, with the right strategies and tactics, you can launch your agency for free and achieve success. This book will guide you through the process of setting up your agency, building your brand, finding clients, and delivering exceptional services, all without spending a dime.

In this book, you'll learn:

1. How to create a solid business plan that outlines your vision, goals, and strategies for success.

2. How to establish your brand identity, including your agency name, logo, and website.

3. How to leverage social media platforms, such as Facebook, Twitter, and Instagram, to market your agency and reach potential clients.

4. How to find and win clients, even if you have no previous experience or portfolio to show.

5. How to deliver high-quality social media marketing services, including content creation, social media management, and analytics.

And much more!

Whether you're a recent graduate, a stay-at-home parent, or an aspiring entrepreneur, this book is for you. By following the advice and insights shared in these pages, you'll be able to launch your social media marketing agency for free and break new ground in the digital marketing industry.

So, get ready to take the first step towards building a successful social media marketing agency. Let's break ground together!

Preface

Congratulations on taking the first step toward launching your own social media marketing agency! This guide, "Launch Your Free Social Media Agency: Breaking Ground," is designed to help you start your journey toward building a successful business that helps others thrive on social media.

In today's digital age, social media has become a vital component of any business's marketing strategy. With the rise of social media platforms like Facebook, Instagram, and Twitter, businesses of all sizes are turning to social media to connect with their audience, build brand awareness, and drive sales. As a result, the demand for social media marketing services has never been higher, presenting an exciting opportunity for aspiring entrepreneurs like you.

But launching a social media marketing agency can be a daunting task, especially if you're just starting out. You may be wondering where to begin, how to find clients, and how to stand out in a crowded market. That's where this guide comes in.

In this guide, we'll walk you through the key steps you need to take to launch your social media marketing agency for free. We'll cover everything from identifying your niche and defining your services to building your brand, finding clients, and scaling your business. We'll provide you with practical tips, real-world examples, and actionable advice that you can implement today.

We wrote this guide with you in mind, with the goal of making it easy and accessible for anyone to start their own social media marketing agency. Whether you're a recent graduate, a stay-at-home parent, or someone looking for a career change, this guide will provide you with the tools and knowledge you need to succeed.

So, let's get started and break new ground on your journey to launching your free social media marketing agency!

Acknowledgements

I am deeply grateful to everyone who has helped me bring this book to life. Your support, encouragement, and guidance have been invaluable.

First and foremost, I want to thank my family and friends for their unwavering belief in me and for cheering me on every step of the way. Your love and encouragement have given me the strength to pursue my dreams, and for that, I will be forever grateful.

I also want to express my sincere appreciation to the team at TR GROUP for providing me with the knowledge and expertise that has made this book possible. Your commitment to advancing the field of artificial intelligence is truly inspiring, and I feel honored to be part of your mission.

I am also grateful to the many individuals who have generously shared their insights and experiences with me. Your stories have provided valuable inspiration and guidance, and I hope that this book will help others as much as it has helped me.

Finally, I want to thank the readers of this book. Your interest in my work and your willingness to learn and grow alongside me is what motivate me to keep going. I hope that this book will inspire you to take the leap and start your own social media marketing agency, and I wish you all the best in your endeavors.

Thank you from the bottom of my heart.

Sincerely,

Tushar Raj

Prologue

Welcome to "Launch Your Free Social Media Agency: Breaking Ground", a comprehensive guide on how to start your very own social media marketing agency without spending money.

In today's digital age, social media is an indispensable tool for businesses of all sizes. From small startups to large corporations, a strong social media presence is crucial for attracting and retaining customers. And that's where social media marketing agencies come in. They help businesses navigate the complex world of social media marketing and achieve their goals through strategic planning, content creation, and data analysis.

Starting your own social media marketing agency can be a daunting task, especially if you're on a tight budget. But fear not! This guide will take you step-by-step through the process of launching your own agency, without spending a single penny.

We'll cover everything from developing your business plan to building your team, from crafting a winning proposal to attracting clients, and from managing your finances to growing your agency.

Whether you're a seasoned social media marketer looking to strike out on your own, or a newbie with a passion for social media and a desire to start your own business, this guide is for you.

So, get ready to break ground and launch your own free social media marketing agency. With this guide as your companion, the sky's the limit!

Prologue

Welcome to "Launch Your [illegible] Breaking Ground", a comprehensive guide [illegible] start [illegible] own social media marketing agency [illegible] spending money.

[illegible] today's digital [illegible] social [illegible] tool for businesses of all sizes. From [illegible] media [illegible]

[illegible]

[illegible] this guide is for you.

[illegible] to break free and launch your own [illegible] With this guide [illegible] the sky's the limit.

Author Info

Tushar Raj

@tusharraj9090

ONE

INTRODUCTION

I. Introduction

Starting your own social media marketing agency can be an exciting and rewarding experience. Not only does it give you the freedom to work for yourself, but it also allows you to help businesses grow their online presence and achieve their marketing goals. In this book, we will explore how to launch your own social media agency, and we'll show you how to do it for free.

II. The benefits of starting a social media marketing agency

There are numerous benefits to starting your own social media marketing agency. For starters, it allows you to take control of your own career and work on your own terms. You'll have the freedom to choose your clients, set your own rates, and decide what kind of work you want to take on.

In addition to the freedom and flexibility, there's also a huge demand for social media marketing services. With the rise of social media and the increasing importance of online marketing, businesses of all sizes are looking for help with their social media presence. As a result, social media marketing is a growing industry that offers plenty of opportunities for those with the right skills and expertise.

III. Why starting for free is a smart choice

While starting a social media agency may sound like an expensive endeavor, it doesn't have to be. In fact, starting for free is a smart choice for a number of reasons. For starters, it allows you to test the waters without taking on a lot of financial risks. You can start small and grow your agency over time, as you start to build a client base and generate revenue.

Starting for free also forces you to be creative and resourceful. When you don't have a lot of money to work with, you have to find ways to make the most of what you have. This can lead to innovative solutions and creative approaches that set you apart from other agencies in the market.

Another benefit of starting for free is that it forces you to be disciplined and focused. When you're not able to rely on a lot of startup capital, you have to be careful about where you invest your time and resources. This can lead to a leaner, more efficient business model that is better equipped to weather the ups and downs of the market.

IV. Conclusion

In this book, we'll show you how to launch your own social media agency for free. We'll cover everything from building your website and branding your agency to attracting clients and scaling your business. By following the advice in this book, you can start your own social media agency and take control of your career without breaking the bank. So let's get started and break ground on your new social media marketing agency!

Exercise: Why Start Your Social Media Marketing Agency for Free?

Starting a business can be expensive, but what if you could launch a successful social media marketing agency without spending a dime? In this exercise, we'll explore the benefits of starting your agency for free and help you decide if it's the right choice for you.

1. List the benefits of starting your social media marketing agency for free. Consider factors such as financial savings, resourcefulness, and flexibility.

2. Reflect on your personal goals and vision for your agency. Do you prioritize making a profit or making an impact? How important is financial security to you? Consider how starting for free may align or conflict with your goals.

3. Research and compare the costs of starting a social media marketing agency with and without paying for resources. Consider the costs of website hosting, social media management tools, advertising, and other necessary expenses.

4. Identify any potential drawbacks or challenges of starting your agency for free. How will you overcome

these challenges and maintain a professional image without investing money upfront?

5. Make a decision on whether to launch your social media marketing agency for free or invest in paid resources. Write down your reasoning and any specific strategies you plan to use to make the most of your free resources.

Remember, starting for free may be a great option for some, but it's not the only path to success. The most important factor is to choose the approach that aligns with your personal goals and vision for your agency.

TWO

UNDERSTANDING SOCIAL MEDIA MARKETING

Social media has revolutionized the way businesses reach and engage with their customers. With millions of people logging onto social media platforms every day, it has become an essential marketing tool for businesses of all sizes. In this chapter, we will explore the role of social media in modern marketing, the benefits of social media marketing for businesses, and the different social media platforms and their unique features.

The Role of Social Media in Modern Marketing

Marketing has always been about reaching the right people, at the right time, with the right message. Social media has become an important part of the modern marketing mix because it allows businesses to do just that. Social media provides a unique opportunity to engage with customers on a more personal level, build brand awareness, and drive sales.

Social media marketing is not just about promoting your products or services. It is about building relationships with your customers and creating a community around your brand. By using social media to engage with your customers, you can gain valuable insights into their preferences and behaviors, and use this information to improve your marketing strategy.

* The Benefits of Social Media Marketing for Businesses

Social media marketing has numerous benefits for businesses, including:

1. Increased brand awareness: Social media platforms are a great way to increase your brand's visibility and reach a wider audience.

2. Improved customer engagement: Social media provides an opportunity to engage with your customers and build a community around your brand.

3. Targeted advertising: Social media advertising allows you to target specific demographics, interests, and behaviors, ensuring that your message reaches the right people.

4. Improved customer service: Social media provides a platform for customers to ask questions, voice concerns, and provide feedback in real-time.

5. Increased website traffic: Social media can be used to drive traffic to your website, improving your search engine rankings and generating more leads.

* The Different Social Media Platforms and Their Unique Features

There are numerous social media platforms available, each with its unique features and advantages. Here are some of the most popular social media platforms and what they are best used for:

1. Facebook: With over 2.8 billion monthly active users, Facebook is the most popular social media platform. It is an excellent platform for businesses to build brand awareness and engage with customers through content, ads, and groups.

2. Instagram: Instagram is a visual platform that is perfect for businesses that want to showcase their products or services through high-quality images and videos. With over 1 billion monthly active users, it is also an excellent platform for influencer marketing.

3. Twitter: Twitter is a fast-paced platform that is perfect for businesses that want to engage with their customers in real-time. It is an excellent platform for customer service, news updates, and driving website traffic.

4. LinkedIn: LinkedIn is a professional networking platform that is ideal for B2B marketing. It is an excellent platform for building business relationships, generating leads, and sharing industry news and insights.

5. TikTok: TikTok is a popular video-sharing platform that is perfect for businesses that want to reach a younger audience. It is an excellent platform for influencer marketing and creating viral content.

In conclusion, social media has become an essential part of modern marketing. It provides businesses with an opportunity to engage with customers on a more personal level, build brand awareness, and drive sales. By understanding the different social media platforms and their unique features, businesses can create an effective social media marketing strategy that delivers results.

Exercise: Identify the Best Social Media Platforms for Your Clients

One of the key steps in understanding social media marketing is knowing which platforms are best for your clients. For this exercise, you'll identify the top social media platforms for three different types of businesses.

1. Start by researching and identifying three different types of businesses. You might choose a local coffee shop, a B2B software company, and a fitness studio.

2. For each business, identify the target audience. Who are they trying to reach? For example, the coffee shop might be targeting young adults and college students, while the B2B software company is targeting IT professionals and decision-makers in businesses.

3. Research and identify the social media platforms that are most popular among each business's target audience. For example, Instagram and TikTok might be popular among the coffee shop's target audience, while LinkedIn and Twitter might be popular among the B2B software company's target audience.

4. Based on your research, create a chart or table that lists the top social media platforms for each business. You

might also include a brief explanation of why each platform is a good fit for that business's target audience.

5. Use your chart or table to help guide your own social media marketing strategy for each client. For example, if you're working with the coffee shop, you might prioritize creating content for Instagram and TikTok, while for the B2B software company, you might focus on LinkedIn and Twitter.

By identifying the best social media platforms for your clients, you'll be able to create more targeted and effective social media marketing campaigns that reach the right audience.

THREE

Building Your Agency for Free

When starting your social media marketing agency for free, it's important to be resourceful and take advantage of all the free tools and resources available. In this chapter, we'll discuss how to build your agency from the ground up without spending a dime.

A. Finding Free Resources for Starting Your Agency

1. Research and Networking

Before starting your social media marketing agency, it's important to research and network with other professionals in the industry. Attend free networking events, connect with professionals on LinkedIn, and join social media marketing groups to gain valuable insights and advice.

2. Open-Source Software

Open-Source Software is a great option for starting your agency for free. These software programs are free to use, and you can modify and distribute them as needed. Popular open-source software programs for social media management include Hootsuite, Buffer, and Canva.

3. Free Web Hosting

To create your agency's website for free, take advantage of free web hosting services like Wix, WordPress, and Weebly. These services provide you with the tools and templates needed to build a professional website without spending any money.

B. Creating a Website, Social Media Profiles, and Branding for Free

1. Website Design

When designing your agency's website, focus on creating a clean and professional design that is easy to navigate. Use free website builders to create a visually appealing website that highlights your services and expertise.

2. Social Media Profiles

Create social media profiles for your agency on the platforms your target audience is most likely to use. Use free tools like Canva to create profile pictures and cover images that match your branding and make a strong first impression.

3. Branding

Creating a strong brand is essential to your agency's success. Utilize free resources like Namechk to check the availability of your desired agency name across social media platforms. Use Canva or other free design tools to create a logo and other branding materials that reflect your agency's personality and expertise.

C. Utilizing Free Tools and Software to Manage Your Agency

1. Social Media Management

To manage your social media accounts for free, use social media management tools like Hootsuite or Buffer. These tools allow you to schedule posts, monitor social media activity, and track analytics across multiple platforms.

2. Project Management

For project management, use free tools like Trello, Asana, or Google Docs to organize and collaborate with team members and clients. These tools allow you to assign tasks, track progress, and communicate with team members and clients in real time.

3. Accounting and Invoicing

To manage your agency's finances, use free accounting and invoicing software like Wave, ZipBooks, or Invoice Ninja. These tools allow you to track income and expenses, create professional invoices, and manage your cash flow.

By utilizing the free resources and tools available, you can build a successful social media marketing agency without spending a dime. In the next chapter, we'll discuss how to attract clients for free and grow your agency organically.

Exercise: Building Your Agency for Free

In this exercise, you'll explore free resources and tools for creating a website, social media profiles, and branding for your agency.

I. Finding Free Resources

Start by searching for free resources online that can help you create your agency. Some websites and platforms to consider include:

1. Canva: a graphic design platform with free templates and tools to create your branding and social media graphics.

2. Google Sites: a free website builder that offers customizable templates and easy-to-use tools.

3. WordPress: a popular free website builder with a wide range of customizable templates and plugins.

4. Hootsuite: a free social media management tool that allows you to manage multiple social media profiles in one place.

II. Creating a Website

Using one of the above free resources, create a simple but professional website for your agency. Make sure to include:

1. An overview of your services and what sets your agency apart

2. A portfolio of your work or case studies

3. Contact information and a way for potential clients to get in touch with you

III. Creating Social Media Profiles

Create social media profiles for your agency on the platforms where your potential clients are most active. Use your branding to create a cohesive look and feel across all platforms. Make sure to include:

1. A bio that clearly explains what your agency does

2. Consistent branding and imagery

3. Relevant hashtags and keywords

IV. Utilizing Free Tools and Software

There are a variety of free tools and software available to help you manage your agency, including:

1. Asana: a free project management tool that allows you to track tasks and deadlines.

2. Trello: a free visual project management tool that allows you to organize tasks in a flexible way.

3. Slack: a free communication tool that allows you to stay in touch with team members and clients.

By utilizing these free resources, you can build a professional and effective agency without breaking the bank. Remember, starting for free doesn't mean your agency can't be successful - it just means you'll need to be creative and resourceful.

FOUR

Attracting Clients for Free

One of the biggest challenges when starting a social media marketing agency is attracting clients. Fortunately, there are several ways you can attract clients for free.

A. Identifying Your Target Audience and Niche

Before you can attract clients, you need to identify your target audience and niche. Your target audience is the group of people or businesses that are most likely to use your services. Your niche is the specific area of social media marketing you specialize in.

To identify your target audience, consider factors such as demographics, industry, and location. For example, if you specialize in social media marketing for small businesses, your target audience may be small business owners in your local area.

To identify your niche, consider the areas of social media marketing you excel or have the most experience. This could be content creation, social media advertising, influencer marketing, or something else.

B. Creating a Portfolio to Showcase Your Skills

Once you've identified your target audience and niche, the next step is to create a portfolio to showcase your skills. Your portfolio should include examples of your work, such as social media posts, ad campaigns, and analytics reports.

If you're just starting out and don't have any client work to showcase, consider creating social media posts and ad campaigns for fictional companies or non-profit organizations. This will give potential clients an idea of your style and approach to social media marketing.

C. Utilizing Free Marketing Strategies to Attract Clients

There are several free marketing strategies you can use to attract clients to your social media marketing agency.

1. Social Media Marketing

The first strategy is social media marketing. Use social media platforms to showcase your portfolio, share industry news and insights, and engage with potential clients. LinkedIn, in particular, can be a great platform for connecting with businesses and professionals in your target audience.

2. Content Marketing

Another strategy is content marketing. Create blog posts, videos, and other content that provides value to your target audience. This could be tips on social media marketing, case studies of successful campaigns, or industry news and trends. Share your content on social media and through email marketing to attract potential clients to your agency.

3. Referral Marketing

Referral marketing is another effective strategy for attracting clients for free. Ask your existing clients and contacts to refer you to their network. Offer incentives for referrals, such as a discount on your services or a referral bonus.

4. Cold Emailing

Finally, cold emailing can be an effective strategy for reaching out to potential clients. Create a list of businesses in your target audience and send them a personalized email introducing your agency and offering your services.

D. Conclusion

Attracting clients for free is a great way to get your social media marketing agency off the ground. By identifying your target audience and niche, creating a portfolio, and utilizing free marketing strategies, you can attract clients and grow your agency without spending a lot of money.

Exercise: Attracting Clients for Free

In this exercise, you'll apply the strategies outlined in the "Attracting Clients for Free" chapter to your own social media marketing agency. By the end of the exercise, you'll have a plan for attracting clients without spending any money.

I. Identify Your Target Audience and Niche

Take some time to think about your target audience and niche. Who are the businesses or individuals you want to work with? What specific area of social media marketing do you specialize in?

Write down your target audience and niche in a clear and specific way. For example, "My target audience is small business owners in the tech industry in the San Francisco Bay Area, and my niche is social media advertising."

II. Create a Portfolio to Showcase Your Skills

Now, it's time to create a portfolio that showcases your skills. Gather examples of your work, such as social media posts, ad campaigns, and analytics reports.

If you don't have any client work to showcase, create social media posts and ad campaigns for fictional companies or non-profit organizations. This will give potential clients an idea of your style and approach to social media marketing.

Organize your portfolio in a way that makes it easy for potential clients to view and understand. Consider creating a website or social media page dedicated to your portfolio.

III. Utilize Free Marketing Strategies to Attract Clients

Next, it's time to start attracting clients for free. Choose one or more of the following free marketing strategies:

1. Social media marketing: Choose one or two social media platforms to focus on, such as LinkedIn or Twitter. Share your portfolio, industry news, and insights, and engage with potential clients. Consider using hashtags and tagging businesses or individuals you want to work with.

2. Content marketing: Create blog posts, videos, or other content that provides value to your target audience. Share your content on social media and through email marketing to attract potential clients to your agency.

3. Referral marketing: Ask your existing clients and contacts to refer you to their network. Offer incentives for referrals, such as a discount on your services or a referral bonus.

4. Cold emailing: Create a list of businesses in your target audience and send them a personalized email introducing your agency and offering your services. Keep your email

brief, professional, and focused on the value you can provide.

IV. Evaluate and Adjust Your Strategy After a few weeks of implementing your free marketing strategy, take some time to evaluate its effectiveness. Look at the engagement and response you've received from potential clients, and make adjustments as needed.

If a particular strategy isn't working, try something else. Don't be afraid to experiment and take risks.

By the end of the exercise, you should have a clear plan for attracting clients for free. Remember, the key is to identify your target audience and niche, create a portfolio that showcases your skills, and utilize free marketing strategies to attract potential clients. Good luck!

FIVE

Scaling Your Free Social Media Agency

Once you've attracted clients and established your social media marketing agency, the next step is to scale and grow your business. Here are some tips for scaling your free social media agency:

A. Identifying Opportunities for Growth and Expansion

The first step in scaling your agency is to identify opportunities for growth and expansion. This could involve expanding your services to include other areas of digital marketing, such as SEO or email marketing, or targeting new industries or markets.

To identify opportunities for growth, consider the needs of your existing clients and the trends in the industry. Attend industry events and conferences, read industry publications and blogs, and network with other professionals to stay up-to-date on the latest trends and opportunities.

B. Utilizing Paid Resources to Enhance Your Agency

While the goal of a free social media marketing agency is to minimize expenses, there are some paid resources that can help enhance your agency and improve your services. These could include paid social media advertising, paid analytics tools, or paid project management software.

When considering paid resources, be sure to weigh the benefits against the cost. Look for tools and services that will provide a significant return on investment and improve the quality of your work.

C. Hiring and Managing a Team of Freelancers or Contractors

As your agency grows, you may need to hire additional staff to manage client accounts and projects. Hiring full-time employees can be expensive, so consider working with freelancers or contractors on a project basis.

When hiring freelancers or contractors, be sure to vet their qualifications and experience, and establish clear expectations and deadlines for their work. Use project management software to ensure that all team members are on the same page and that projects are completed on time and on budget.

D. Conclusion

Scaling a free social media marketing agency requires careful planning, strategic decision-making, and a willingness to invest in resources and talent when necessary. By identifying opportunities for growth, utilizing paid resources, and working with freelancers and contractors, you can take your agency to the next level and continue to provide high-quality services to your clients.

Exercise - Scaling Your Free Social Media Agency

Once you've attracted clients and built a successful social media marketing agency for free, it's time to think about scaling your business. Here's an exercise to help you identify opportunities for growth and expansion, and develop a plan to take your agency to the next level.

I. Identify Opportunities for Growth

The first step is to identify opportunities for growth and expansion. Consider the following questions:

1. Are there new services or niches you could offer to your existing clients?

2. Are there new target audiences you could reach with your services?

3. Are there new social media platforms or marketing channels you could utilize?

Q. Write down your answers to these questions and brainstorm additional ideas for growth and expansion.

II. Assess Your Resources

Once you've identified opportunities for growth, the next step is to assess your resources. Consider the following questions:

1. What resources do you currently have available (e.g. time, money, skills)?

2. What resources will you need to achieve your growth goals?

3. How will you acquire or access these resources?

Q. Write down your answers to these questions and develop a plan to acquire or access the resources you need.

III. Develop a Growth Plan

Once you've identified opportunities for growth and assessed your resources, the next step is to develop a growth plan. Your growth plan should include the following:

1. Specific goals and targets for growth (e.g. increasing revenue by 50%, expanding into a new niche)

2. Strategies for achieving your growth goals (e.g. offering new services, reaching out to new target audiences, utilizing new marketing channels)

3. A timeline for implementing your growth strategies (e.g. which strategies will you implement first, how long will each strategy take to implement)

4. Key performance indicators (KPIs) to measure your progress towards your growth goals (e.g. revenue, client retention, social media engagement)

Q. Write down your growth plan and review it regularly to track your progress and adjust your strategies as needed.

IV. Hire and Manage a Team

As your agency grows, you may need to hire and manage a team of freelancers or contractors to help you manage client work and achieve your growth goals. Consider the following questions:

1. What roles and responsibilities will you need to hire for?

2. What skills and experience will your team members need?

3. How will you find and hire team members?

4. How will you manage and communicate with your team members?

Q. Write down your answers to these questions and develop a plan for hiring and managing a team.

By completing this exercise, you'll be well on your way to scaling your free social media marketing agency and achieving your growth goals. Remember to stay flexible and adaptable as you grow, and to continue utilizing free resources and strategies to keep your costs low

Notes

9 798889 757047

Printed by Libri Plureos GmbH in Hamburg,
Germany